I CAN DO IT!

I CAN WRITE A LETTER

by Susan Ashley

Photographs by Gregg Andersen

Reading consultant: Susan Nations, M.Ed., author/literacy coach/consultant

WEEKLY WR READER®
EARLY LEARNING LIBRARY

Please visit our web site at: www.earlyliteracy.cc
For a free color catalog describing Weekly Reader® Early Learning Library's
list of high-quality books, call 1-877-445-5824 (USA) or 1-800-387-3178 (Canada).
Weekly Reader® Early Learning Library's fax: (414) 336-0164.

Library of Congress Cataloging-in-Publication Data

Ashley, Susan.
    I can write a letter / by Susan Ashley.
      p. cm. — (I can do it!)
    Includes bibliographical references and index.
    ISBN 0-8368-4328-2 (lib. bdg.)
    ISBN 0-8368-4335-5 (softcover)
    1. Letter writing—Juvenile literature. 2. English language—Composition and
exercises—Juvenile literature. I. Title. II. I can do it! (Milwaukee, Wis.)
    PE1483.A84   2004
    808.6—dc22   2004045133

This edition first published in 2005 by
Weekly Reader® Early Learning Library
330 West Olive Street, Suite 100
Milwaukee, WI 53212 USA

Editor: JoAnn Early Macken
Graphic Designer/Illustrator: Melissa Valuch
Art Director: Tammy West
Picture Researcher: Diane Laska-Swanke
Photographer: Gregg Andersen

Printed in the United States of America

1 2 3 4 5 6 7 8 9 08 07 06 05 04

Note to Educators and Parents

Reading is such an exciting adventure for young children! They are beginning to integrate their oral language skills with written language. To encourage children along the path to early literacy, books must be colorful, engaging, and interesting; they should invite the young reader to explore both the print and the pictures.

I Can Do It! is a new series designed to help young readers learn how ordinary children reach everyday goals. Each book describes a different task that any child can be proud to accomplish.

Each book is specially designed to support the young reader in the reading process. The familiar topics are appealing to young children and invite them to read — and re-read — again and again. The full-color photographs and enhanced text further support the student during the reading process.

In addition to serving as wonderful picture books in schools, libraries, homes, and other places where children learn to love reading, these books are specifically intended to be read within an instructional guided reading group. This small group setting allows beginning readers to work with a fluent adult model as they make meaning from the text. After children develop fluency with the text and content, the book can be read independently. Children and adults alike will find these books supportive, engaging, and fun!

— Susan Nations, M.Ed., author, literacy coach, and consultant in literacy development

I can write a letter.
I can write a letter
to my grandma.

I find a pencil. I find a clean sheet of paper.

I begin my letter with a greeting.

greeting

Dear Grandma,

I tell my grandma about my trip. I tell her what I did at the beach.

I end the letter with a closing. I write my name below it.

We floated and swam.
We played in the sand.
Dave and I had so much
fun in the water!
I'll see you soon.

Love,

Tammy

closing

I fold the letter. I put it in an envelope.

My mother helps me address the envelope.

I put a stamp on the envelope. The stamp has a picture on it.

Now I can mail the letter. I put it in a mailbox. My grandma will be happy to get it!

last collection
6 15
PM
monday thru saturday

UNITED STATES
POSTAL SERVICE

Glossary

address — to write a name and a place on the front of an envelope

closing — the words that end a letter

greeting — the words that begin a letter

mailbox — a box where people put letters that are ready to be mailed. Letters from the mailbox are taken to the Post Office. Then mail carriers deliver them.

For More Information

Books

A Day with a Mail Carrier. Hard Work (series). Jan Kottke (Children's Press)

Dear Annie. Judith Caseley (Greenwillow)

Mail Carrier. People in My Community (series). JoAnn Early Macken (Weekly Reader Early Learning Library)

Messages in the Mailbox: How to Write a Letter. Loreen Leedy (Holiday House)

Web Sites

Letter Generator
readwritethink.org/materials/letter_generator/
Write your own letter and print it

Index

About the Author

Susan Ashley has written more than twenty-five books for children. She has lived all over the United States and in Europe. Thanks to her travels, she has become very good at reading maps and writing letters. She also likes making — and eating — sandwiches. Susan lives in Wisconsin with her husband and two cats. The cats like it when she makes tuna sandwiches!